AROUND THE
RED LAND

NEWFOUNDLAND POETRY SERIES

Larry Small

BREAKWATER

BREAKWATER BOOKS LTD.
100 Water Street P.O. Box 2188 St. John's, NL A1C 6E6
www.breakwaterbooks.com

LIBRARY AND ARCHIVES CANADA CATALOGUING IN PUBLICATION

Small, Larry, 1941-
  Around the Red Land / Larry Small.
(Newfoundland Poetry Series)

ISBN 978-1-55081-235-0
    I. Title. II. Series.
PS8637.M35A66 2007   C811'.6   C2007-900314-1

We acknowledge the financial support of The Canada
Council for the Arts for our publishing activities.

The Canada Council | Le Conseil des Arts
for the Arts | du Canada

We acknowledge the support of the Department of
Tourism, Culture and Recreation for our publishing
activities.

We acknowledge the financial support of the
Government of Canada through the Book Publishing
Industry Development Program (BPIDP) for our
publishing activities.

Canada

Printed in Canada.

Acknowledgements

I would like to thank the following for their many attempts at trying to convince me to take my lines beyond the kitchen table, although many times I questioned their wisdom: John N. Smith, the Montreal filmmaker, who is a master at the art of persuasion; Gerry Squires, whose celestial voice is to be taken seriously; Rex Brown, who often showed his frustration at my many hesitations, but was always generous with his smiles; and Des Walsh, who many times argued with all of his Irish Catholic passion. It was, however, his performance in front of company in his room at the Glynmill Inn that sealed my fate. There was no retreat! I also thank him for editorial advice across many kitchen tables when wine and music seemed to solve the problems of the world.

Al Pittman's friendship was always an inspiration; his melodious voice, as ubiquitous as the clouds, drifting along, never to be dampened by the Humber River.

My sincere thanks to Pat Byrne, the real wizard of Oz, for whom no problem was insurmountable, whether it was the technicalities of language or computer technology. His hearty laugh was always followed by a solution in six seconds or less.

Clyde Rose of Breakwater Books deserves special mention for his courage in bringing my lines to the public domain.

To my daughter, Lori, I owe a deep gratitude for her nerve and willingness to read a final version of my manuscript that would portray to her, for the first time, a world alien in the extreme.

To Valerie Sooley I owe much appreciation for attempting to explain to me the workings of a computer. To someone who only mastered a three horsepower Acadia and a four horsepower Atlantic engine, this was a monumental task. But with sound advice I managed to type my lines although I expected them to disappear at any moment. I will never trust a computer, however, the way I trusted the 'make and break,' or even horses. Only your patience kept me sane, and possibly only your strong belief in what I was doing kept you answering my calls.

for Lori & Valerie

THE BAY FROM LONG POINT

Families climbed the cliffs in June
To watch the schooners round Cape John,
But now, no schooners sing the song of fish.
The southwest wind blows down from Fridays Bay
But finds no trapmen on the grounds,
The berths without their moorings,
Their names vanishing from the lexicon.
The Old Sow weeps
While Western Head stands vigil
To the sea and ice.
And what about the winds...
Are they lonely now
Since those who knew the nuance
Of every breeze
Have shipped into another life?
Who will be a soulmate to the wind
And who will give benediction
To the Bay?

WHICH WAY THE WIND BLOWS

How well they knew the names of winds
That wound their mouths
Around their daily lives
Of work and play
Of twisted fingers
And backs that bore the burdens,
Too much for mortal man.
No phantom this,
Uncensored force beyond the land and sea
That they had learned from childhood…
The compass and the weatherglass.
They knew the rules and menus
Of maddening storms,
Their souls attune to sunsets
Of a thousand years,
And skies at night
When moons made love to earth
And dippers with their handles bent
Bade them look up
And listen to their tunes.
To orchestras of winds
They knew the language and the notes
And often sang the litany
Of lessons long ago,
(*East be Nold / East nold East*)
The dictum of its ways.

The drying winds for fish and clothes
And easterlies with rains for fields
And wells that bore the brunt
Of summer suns.
For glutted fish
They prayed to the north,
And to the south
To shift the ice from land.
To lift the burden
From their master's hand
The horses played their music with the wind
And wound themselves in empty fields,
Helpmates for the weather.

THE UPSTAIRS WINDOW

Through the bedroom window
We looked into the eye of the universe
And saw everything from genesis until now.
Houses and flakes and fish rooms
And the tides tormenting the ocean.
The bees of spring,
Busy among the apple blossoms
Of trees planted by men and women
Who are now only faded memories.
The women who worked the flakes
In summer,
Their souls and sexuality
Wrapped in the obsidian fabrics
Covering their tired and working bodies.
The moon terrified the night
As it played with the sea
Or crept over clumpers of ice…
Among rocks and trees
The walls of bedrooms,
The pages of unread books;
Bore down on tired horses
Tied to winter fences,
Eating hay from gardens fast asleep.
Through the same window
Came the songs of birds,
The blasts from ships' horns,
The cry of howling dogs in the dark.
Macabre scenes of men and women

Walking to churches,
Their dignity descending around the harbour.
When death came to visit,
The ghostly sounds of church bells
Tolling in their anguish,
Flags at half-mast
And blinds bending down on windows
Weeping in their sorrow.
Without those windows in the sky
We cling to the hills and headlands
To heal the darkness of the soul.

DOWN TO THE GUNNELS

They were boats of many metres,
Built by men whose hands
Knew suant lines,
Their white and ochre bodies,
All summer long
Sliced through translucent seas.
The catch of cod from traps
Twelve fathoms down,
Within the lexicon of trapmen
A waterhaul, a tuck of fish.
The man who held the tiller
Hid his pride,
But parents and the children knew
The currency of cod,
Singing out the songs of fish
To those too old for boats,
But knew the anguish of no fish
And came outside
To watch the boats come in.
From the lungers of the stage
Came melodies from long ago
As men moved forward for the view
Of sights they never tire,
The fear of want had disappeared today
The carols of Christmas could admit another child.

THE FISHERMAN

for Chris O'Neill Yates

It's that time of year again
Between summer and fall
When the west winds of September
Sing out their seasonal chorus
Of changing leaves,
And gardens green with the fruits
Of spring and summer.
He surveys the universe,
Decides it's a 'good day on fish.'
But only he
A lifetime treading flakes
Knows what a good day means.
He lifts rinds from cone-shaped
Piles of dried cod,
A yaffle of fish
Lodged in his forearm,
Moves slowly along the flake
Then, one by one,
Spreads fish...
Face to the sky, back to the sea,
Back to the sky, face to the sea
Until the flake is flush with fish...
Rows of black, white and gold.
It's a solemn moment,
Final judgements on his work,
Traded in the market-place
For food and fishing gear

To pay the church,
To pay the doctor.
The oligarchs admonish his children,
Their father's work
A thing of shame.
But he is an artist and
Connoisseur of cod...
Gifts at Christmas,
And at Thanksgiving,
Prime fish displayed
Around communion rails
But never in the eateries
Of his homeland.
He knows the Iberian people
Partake of bacalhau with oils
From their olive groves,
But he did not know
That in Lisbon and Oporto
The Portuguese place his salt cod on a pedestal
With fine wines from their vineyards,
Celebrated with ceremonies of high cuisine
And messages from the cross.
As you and all the men
Who fished with you
Sleep among the blueberry bushes
At the top of the Three Hills,
I bring you news;
That we have moved from shame to greed,

Ravished the sea,
Polluted the ocean with our new technologies,
And endured insults from the oligarchs
Degrading your knowledge
Of fish and the sea.
Not bad after five hundred years.

I wonder what you would say to us?

LABRADOR LOVE

You came from good stock
On the eastern end of the island,
Lulled by men who fished the Labrador
And like the schooners,
Your suant and statuesque body
Occupied the minds of men
Gathered on roads to yarn
On Sundays and summer evenings.
In silence, they watched you
Working on flakes
And holding the flesh of fish
In stages built by those in their prime.
Your beauty transfixed young men
Who viewed the contours of your body
While you gave them ice cream
In cones as big as headlands.

In the long winters of long ago
Your kitchen was the concert hall
On the eastern side of the harbour…
Always visitors playing cards,
Cutting and chewing tobacco
And moving spittoons with animation
As talk roamed around the room
About fish and storms and schooners,
Seals and ice and horses.
Young men and women heard reviews of grandparents
They never knew,
Had never seen a photograph.

What is it like today, living alone,
Looking out on harbours covered in darkness
In the dead of night
With chimneys screaming out for smoke;
On harbours that were once robust with rodneys,
Schooners with sails
And horses moving with the gracefulness
Of westerly clouds?
With no fog horns moaning under a hazy moon,
Or flakes of salt cod spreading its smell and yellow hue
From east to west
While people sit around in stores and stageheads
Sharing the infinite knowledge of their universe?

I hope you are comforted by the mountains
And meadows of hay never mown;
The moon always rising over the 'scrape'
Making the harbour magic in winter,
Turning apple blossoms to apparitions in spring.
That you can listen to the sounds of the sea,
Watch the wind play with the water
And wonder at the morning and evening skies.

Today you surround yourself with pictures
From a lost world,
Your telephone and TV.
You visit the sick and the dead.
Your steps are slower now,
Your body bent,

But your smile and sense of humor
Are still intact
Murmuring every now and then,
'I don't know what it's all about.'

SUNDAY MORNING

You pulled your frail body
Along a grassy slope
Between the highway and the fence
That housed your land.
In that private space,
Attired in dark coat and hat
You moved with your white cane
Carrying a smile as old as the icons
At the altar of your faith.
I wondered where you were going.
Then out of the bright southwest
Radiance of a Sunday morning
I heard the faint bells of St. Peter's.
As the single sound
Became louder and louder,
So did the caricatures
Of all the years your body
Languished along the same path,
Your faith still intact.

GOOD FRIDAY

Good Friday, always silent,
The March sun expanding
Out of the bowels of Wild Cove,
Moving above the Quare and Middle Mountain,
Across the frigid harbour
Towards the Methodist and the Church of England.
There was always church,
The dark solemn figures, like migrating animals,
Treading slowly towards their place of prayer
And then with reverence reserved
For crosses and communion rails,
Feasted on salted herring
Without a murmur,
Never asking why.
Nor did they ask about the deafening silence,
Or why they went fishing
On Big Pond and Little Pond
Or why they thought throwing out dish-water
Assaulted the face of Christ.
I believe that they were afraid of making noise.

THE PARLOUR

The parlour held the seasons on its walls and windows.
The sun's rays, filtered through trees,
Making their own soliloquys,
While ghostly moonbeams moved over
Mantelpieces bent with a backload of history
And on reluctant lovers who would be lovers forever.
The wall-papered walls with floral designs
Reaching back to the Renaissance
Penetrating the intruder
Each time he unlocked the austere door.
The walls mused with family mythologies…
A large foreboding picture of a distant uncle,
Lost at sea off the Spanish coast;
Somber portraits of uncles from the First World War,
My father's grammar school picture
And diploma, Malden, 1925.
Furniture from the Dark Ages
Lugged from America,
Sitting on carpets made for mausoleums
While in a distant corner, a Victrola,
Occasionally belting out the voice of Harry Lauder.
It's here we celebrated Christmas,
The tree standing 'till Easter
Rolled its eggs from barrels of flour.
Thereafter, only death unlocked the door
And the parlour put on its macabre face
Greeting men and women
Who sat for hours
Struggling with their own souls.

NOT A TAYLOR LEFT ON TAYLOR'S ROOM

Two centuries ago, with their West Country ways,
Your people built homesteads around rock and sea…
Stages erected on cliffs
Struggled to stay anchored to the ocean
While houses rose above the high water mark
And the edifice to their religion –
The grand workmanship of their own hands –
Towered toward the sky.
They made love here amidst the roar of the ocean
Around the Red Land
As ghostly light from lighthouses
Shone through the snow dwyes of fall
And foghorns moaned in foggy springs
And full moons rose over Sligo Shore,
Shedding light on cemeteries that held their people.
They practiced their faith here, Church of England,
And raised daughters whose beauty
Transcended the translucent sea
But eluded the raptures of men of other faiths,
Blinded by their own religion.
With trapskiffs from their master builders
They fished nearby grounds
And all their lives crafted salt cod
With the care and beauty of a Van Gogh.
But when the markets, and the merry-making men
Of money, graft and greed
Lifted salt cod from its kosher world,

Their stages fell from the landscape.
Their sons and daughters moved on to other lands
Leaving their kindred to wither
From the earth that bore them.

THE SUNDAY GATHERING

They gathered on Sundays after the noon-day meal
Men in suits and half suits, ties and without ties
And shoes that were blackened on Saturday nights.
One man, smoking, sitting alone on a large rock,
Always the first to arrive, always sitting on the same rock,
Then joined by another and another until the rock is full.
Some men stand while others sit on wharves and flakes
Or abandoned schooners' spars.
They've done this all the civil summer Sundays
Of their lives
As humanity everywhere goes looking for itself.
Cod is the crucible of their lives and all afternoon
They chat about fish caught,
Spread out on flakes or in stores and stages
And always minute detail about the ocean,
Boats and weather.
They move around the roads and wharves
Expressing points of view with waving arms,
Voices modulated by the wind or sometimes
People in windows.
They realize their vulnerability,
Chasing elusive fish at low prices,
Depending on merchants and markets for their living
And here they settle no scores.
But it is their only forum for the summer,
The only forum for the rest of their lives.

THE FOUNDERING STAGE

As the Second World War
Groaned to a close
Men with horses and morning snows
Hauled logs
To lay your foundation in the landwash.
And amidst the sounds of rocks
Anchoring your roots to the sea,
Of axes erasing the years from high timber,
And pit saws making intrusions
Into the souls of juniper and black spruce,
Of wooden spikes
Entering holes still warm from the augers bore,
You gradually rose above the high water mark
Making your own shadows
Between earth and sky on the outside
And on the inside,
A diffuse light without shadows
Where the men who erected this edifice
Made fish.
Throughout the eternity of their lives
You sheltered them,
You listened to the sounds of water
Pouring itself over new blood,
The sounds of salt
Laid on dead fish,
Each fighting its own battles into oblivion.
You heard the talk of tired men
Late at night

When the sky was black,
Moving in their own shadows,
Listening to them when they did not talk,
The silence eclipsed by soundbones
Torn from warm flesh
And fed to the sea.
Now you are lonely for boats
To rub against your loins
Making ghostly sounds on stormy nights,
For footsteps you could always name,
Your heart hurting
For those who have left you.
Soon you will fall into the sea
And seek sanctuary
With those who kept you warm.

THE CULLER

The northwesterlies flung their virginity
Upon the headlands
Moving mantles of white and blue
Throughout the universe
Apologizing for the sadness of summer.
It's September,
And as schools adjudicate the young
The culler starts his solitary judgements
Of a summer's catch
From the easels of boughs and lungers
Where men of might
And women of will have toiled
All summer
With their only stock of trade.
He knows the fish killers,
Their reputation for 'making fish,'
But in the market-place,
With a keen eye and
A gentle hand
He must, without deliberation,
Pass judgements,
(A crucible for jurisprudence)
On fish that will please
The Portuguese, the Spanish, the Italians and the Greeks.
A tall order,
But a wrong hand could extinguish
The fires of love
Or keep food from hungry stomachs
In the dead of winter.
Will it be the stoicism of the Greeks,
Or a scrummage?

JUNE MORNING

One year ago
It was five thirty
On a June morning.
So virginal, so holy.
The birds had made their matins,
Probably a rehearsal for their morning tunes
Reminding us of our humanity
And beckoning us to forget
Many of our own creations
Camouflaging the soul,
Divorcing us from the wild flowers
And the west wind
Moving among the sunlight and shadows
Of a new day
Before the streets are awake
With the roar of their own importance.
But it is always the nexus
Of the natural universe,
Without beseeching,
That rescues Sligo's derelicts
From their insipid world,
Pitching them amongst the winds and willows
Where they holler at the moon
And listen to the cadence
Of the sea at night
Testing its phosphorescence
Before flinging themselves towards the milky way
Giving their vespers to the gods.

RIVERMAN

You stood amongst the trees
On the edge of the river,
Your lean frame
Covered with shirt, headband
And faded cut-off denims
Exposing enough of your wasting body
To remind us of your mortality.
The unkind disease
Had ended your ability to speak
(writing down your responses to our foolish questions)
But you mesmerized us
With your zest for life,
Building your tilt
That you were making into a temple.
You offered us home brew
And showed us the land you cleared,
Moving large trees
With your 'come along'
Alone in the forest
As you erected the floors and walls
Of your temple
Before the frost came.
In your absence
We heard that you might not see
Another Christmas;
Your only money,
What your aged mother
Gave you for food

And the sustenance you gathered
From the fruits of the forest.
On a back road
We saw your old van
But we hope you did not see us
Looking into your secret space
As we read on yet another piece of paper,
"Bild road to river."

THE DROWNING AT NINE MILE POND

You stood against the bar
Smiling, without saying much,
Enjoying an evening beer.
Your hands and face of steel
Gave messages of half a century
Of encounters with the landscape
Of your birth.
At mid-winter, news came
That you had drowned
At Nine Mile Pond
Only a few miles from your home,
Only a few miles from where I first met you.

In the dark, cold night
You and your machine
Battled the icy waters,
Your 'working hands' bleeding, torn,
Your shivering body finally receding
Into the freezing waters of the black night.
They found you in the muddy deeps
Forty-five feet down
And slowly brought you
To your final trip on Nine Mile Pond.

Your family long dispersed,
Your house facing the harbour in deadly silence
Comforted only by the truck standing
Inside your garden,
All wondering where you were,
You who knew Nine Mile
Like the palm of your hand.

THE LOST LOVER

As a young man you worked the river
At the bottom of Third Pond
Among the elite of the banker's world,
Among skilled rivermen, craftsmen, woodsmen
Who knew hunger and hard work,
Some could not write their name.
Today you headed downstream
Consumed by one thought,
Tonight you were marrying a woman from your bay.
To ward off the chill of a salt water spring,
Men who lit fires for centuries
Warmed the church halls
As women prepared food for the wedding feast
And readied the church for men in dark suits
And women in many coloured dresses.
You dear bride, three months with child
And dressed for the occasion of your life,
Stood at the mouth of the river
Nervously waiting for your man.
Journeying downstream among men in other boats
Your man was celebrating the rest of his life.
As the riverboats left the fresh water
And languished among the ice pans
Of a north Atlantic spring
A challenge was issued in the race for shore.
Your lover did not make it.
The ocean received his boat and body,
His soul rests among the ballicatters and a broken bride.

LOVE AND DEATH

You came when the cold hand of death
Was half way in the door.
Your green eyes and angular face
A gift to those who grieved
As you moved with the west wind
Caressing the harbour,
The west wind caressing your soul.
Your body pulsated with the seasons…
The prismatic colours of sun on snow,
The sounds of the sea's embrace
As it wove its arms around the headlands,
Kissing the sand and beach rocks
With its turquoise tongue;
Moonbeams moving over trees
That tried to sleep
On February nights,
On beaver houses bedded down for winter.
You transcended the mythologies
Of those who sought to silence your soul,
To crush the music from your heart,
Climbing mountains by day,
Orion's orbit at night.
Your messianic body
Moved among the medical wards
In the low lights of lonely nights
When hope was only an infant.
Your hands held lovers throughout eternity…

Serenaded them in their joy and sadness,
But now left in their loneliness forever
As they watched the wakes of ships
Taking you back to genesis,
To motherhood,
To the serpentine mineral
That slowed your writing hand,
That took you in your bloom.

YOUR NINE FATHOM TRAP

In the night of a northwest wind
Death took you in your prime
Leaving your family numb with sadness
And alone in their solitude
As they navigated a strange new world
Among those who sought to help lives
That did not want to keep on living.
And in this solemn season
Men from the harbour
Want your nine fathom trap.
"It's so easy to move among berths," they say.
"You're not getting it for a song,"
Intoned a cousin in charge.
As seasoned fishermen under run armfuls of twine
In the damp and dreary silence
Of a fall's fish store
He thinks of you resting
Among the fading leaves of October.
He feels very much alone in his grief
Grasping for the first time
That death does not assassinate
A peoples' greed.

SHOALS OF CAPLIN

The shoals of caplin, male and female,
Moved through the blue-green water
At the end of their pilgrimage of love and lust
Resting their spawn upon the sand and rocks.
All the years of your working life
You waited for them,
Standing stoic at the edge of the ocean,
The silence broken by the sea
Caressing the shoreline
And the music of your feet upon the beach.
Like a hound, silhouetted among the headlands
You made your move,
Swinging your castnet
Among the small, silver fish,
Their streamlined bodies
Erupting into contortions of madness
Until with resignation
They acknowledged death.

PLANTING THE POTATOES
for Ross Traverse

Each spring you sat there by the Alexander
Meticulously cutting seed for a new crop of potatoes...
Minions, Fortyfolds, Irish Cobblers,
Arron Victories and the Blues.
Like a new moon,
You did not announce those days,
But driven by some primordial promise
To set your gardens.
And there, with fertilizers of fish and kelp,
Dropped your seed in the open
Wounds of the warm earth.
No messenger sang out at midday
Only your solitary voice,
'there's a scattered potato coming up.'
In the secrets of our souls we felt good
But never said so.
And when we viewed a medley of flowers
Moving with the west wind,
We longed for the October harvest
Among the fading colors of fall
Filling the cellars with reds, whites and blues
'Cause you got nothing if you got no potatoes.'

THE MOWER

Your house watched over the north Atlantic
And your garden of well cut grass,
Fenced in with years of caring.
Now your body suffers from the years
Of love and work and angst
Your step has slowed,
Your torso twisted by the wind and rain.
Today you step outside your fence,
Abandoning your walker
While your lover holds the back of your pants
Wondering about her life with you,
The mower,
As you swing your scythe
Into this year's growth
Compelled by forces beyond Cupid's reach.

THE BERRY PICKERS

They came in punts and rodneys,
Sleek, white boats
With ochre and tarred bottoms
Propelled by nubile men and women
And those worn by the years
Pulling the weight of their bodies
With paddles crafted without crucifix.
This was the Angelus of autumn
When westerly winds gave permission
For the pilgrimage
Among fading leaves
And skies of white and blue.
They climbed the mountains,
Single file,
Ghostlike in the heavens
Away from open doors and windows
Where the hills cried out in their horniness.
They dragged their bodies
From berry patch to berry patch
Caressing the pungent fruit of fall.
When evening came
They descended the high hills,
Bags of berries hanging from backs
Tired from the elixirs of the day
Making their journey into winter…
For they were the Church of England
From the other side,
Never admitting
They were just like us.

THE BLACKSMITH

You were a contrary bastard,
Playing your blacksmith's role
With your sardonic wit
Against the wise, the worshippers
And Zeus.
Was this because you always
Stroked the fires of hell,
Your hands pumping the bellows
While your eyes held unto Hyades,
Or because you worked with
Wayward horses?
'Balky bastards,' you said,
As you moulded the molten metal
To fit the hooves of stallions
And of mares.
The gaff hooks and the grapnels
Gave you pause,
As did the skegs of boats,
But while the wheelwright
Always wore the smile
And men in midship-rooms
Mourned the lack of space,
All year long your face
Welled up with guile.

THE WINTER MAILMAN
for Warwick Horwood

They lived their lives with wind and tides
Sleet and snow and storms
With moons and moaning ice
The sky at dusk and dawn,
The sky in the dark night.
They knew the subtleties of winds
The wanderings of clouds
The bent of trees
The silence of a horse's stare.
Their horses worked the gardens and the woods,
The sick to doctors in the dead of night
The dead unto their place of rest.
To walk or run
With slides and sleds
The sweat of heavy loads,
All this they knew
And with reverence and respect
Called out the horse's name.
The people knew that horsemen
Were a different breed,
The news was safe with them,
The clothes at Christmas
The catalogues of spring and fall.
And when bells rang out
From the noble beast,
The mouths of centuries moved in chorus,
'The mail is come.'

Waiting in waiting rooms,
Men and women
With grace and nervous smiles
Yarned among themselves
As if a child was born
Until the wickets opened wide
On withering sun and snow.

GOING DOWN TO SEE THE DOCTOR

They were strangers to the world of medicine,
Once a lifetime,
Maybe never,
But tonight they tapped the weatherglass,
'Sized up' the sky and which way the wind blew.
Tomorrow it was Twillingate, to see the doctor.
Six miles by boat in open season,
Twelve miles by a different route
In the dead of winter on horses travelling trails
Through woods and over frozen bays
Their shadows moving with the sun and moon
And music from their bells among the ice and trees.
Or from the midship-rooms of boats,
The music from the 'make and breaks'
Moaning in the early morning hour
Moving headlands in its wake
Until the hospital towers loomed
Like monuments of death.

Inside the ominous doors to the OPD
They sat and stared at faces worn by the wind,
Chatting and smoking pipes
As the restless ones driven by their angst
Rang bells to call the nurses with the news
Of when they would get inside to see the doctor.
Inside they sat in stalls of silence,
Wet hands and trembling heart
Until their bodies bore the rubber mallets,

Scopes back and forth,
And gave the lineage of their lives.
Sometimes these foreign souls were led to wards
Where they were slain by sarcastic voices
Or endured the odious smells of ether,
Their only comfort Mr. Ings, the orderly.

Released to the outside world
They rose from the long benches
Tired and red-faced,
Bidding farewell to friends.
Out through the door,
The melodic chant of more names called
Fading as they moved down the steps
Among the roar of sea or blinding snow,
Freedom's gift of home.

ODE TO JOHN LOCKE

You were the icon of the great Sicilian,
Son of Titus,
Tall, broad shouldered, red faced,
Expansive girth,
Covered always with dark suits
And sometimes a long gold chain
Going to the pocket of your vest.
Your house, always with a warm
And busy kitchen,
Lodged only a few feet
From the high water mark
And there, through northern windows,
One viewed the relics
Of your family's past,
The last schooner that took you
To the Labrador.
After your parents
Went to the cemetery by Second Pond
You lived alone
And celebrated the long days
With holy ritual.
Sunday mornings, in dark pants and white shirt,
You did honour to yourself
And those before you
As the smells from fish and brewis
Spread itself throughout the universe.
And no matter where you were,
Working hard like your friends

And the rest of your family,
Or enjoying days of long drinks,
You were always the noblest of men
From the Northeast.
Your reverent phrase, 'yes, my son,'
Came forth a million times in your manhood
And forever received with quiet dignity.
In the rough weather of fall and winter
People from the Island's west side
Brought their sick for you
To transport to the hospital in Twillingate,
You the trusted mariner
You the trusted horseman.

You would visit us three miles away
And sit with my father and other men
Throughout the day and night
Talking the long talks of worlds
Beyond my feeble youth and drink the beers
That only fathers made.
But you came in your glory
Of dress and horse gear
When you paraded with the Orangemen in March.
You and your friends came by mid-morning
And entered your horses in waiting stables
And ate and drank and talked
'Till the rituals of your Order
Called forth to march the harbour ice.

Sometimes you did not go home
But lay your large body
On the kitchen couch
And did your heavy breathing
Until dawn.

I last saw you
On a chilly September morning
Sitting by yourself
Outside a place for people of your age,
Now fifty miles from home.
Still red faced,
With pipe somewhere between hand and mouth,
You told me stories
And said that soon you would
Go down and dig your potatoes
Before the frost came,
Then asked me in for a drink.
And there, displaced and discarded
By the new regime,
You did not curse the heavens
Nor complain because
You were still alone.

FIRST SNOW

Last night the snow came,
Spreading its blanket on our innocence
Making us accountable again
As it knocked on doors
Looked into our eyes
Daring us to come outside.
But the city doesn't give a damn
About your innocence,
You have come with your web of misery.
Long ago you came to horses newly shod
Forcing us to wonder...
The shape of horses' hooves,
The width of slides,
The print of men in mogs
Or snow-shoed feet,
Or lovers on the loose;
The tracks of fox and rabbit
Muskrat, beaver, bird.
The universe was alive again
Dancing our DNA
Before our very eyes.

THE HUNT

That night on Rushy Pond Road
When the moon and stars touched the earth
And you and your companions
Gathered among the first snows of winter
Caressing each other's bodies
Feasting on last year's birch,
You did not know
Twentieth century man
Lurked with his deadly arsenal.
This would be your
Last night of love
Your last winter's dawn.
At eight you stood alone at bogside
Separated from your friends of two years
When you entered the cross-hairs
Of the hunter's scope
And became a victim of
Man's massacre for meat.
Lying now in the quiet snows
Of a late November morning
Your blood gave cinema to
The silent bog
Hanging on half-dead trees
Seeping into young snows
Oozing from your fatal wound
As if your heart was still working.

All that day men would
Celebrate your death
Drink to their health
Dissect your body
With the skill of a surgeon's scalpel
Freeze the flesh of your body
And then give grace.

LONG POINT CALLING CAPE JOHN
for Shannon Ryan

When we were still our own country
The schooner brought the freight one fall,
And families waited for the wonders of the wireless
As those West Countrymen strung wires to grumps
To give the voice of radio
Unto the sea and sky.
The kitchen waited, with shelves set out with linen,
And wires to poles from westard path
So they could listen to the lighthouse keeper's voice
Spread out along the northeast grid
And from ships they had never seen.
The chorus of names from maps now came alive...
Belle Isle and Bacalhao,
Cape John, Long Point,
The Penguins and the Wadhams.
On winter nights, all working men sat still
And listened to the keepers and their code:
"Twillingate Long Point calling Cape John Gull Island"
"Twillingate Long Point calling Cape John Gull Island"
"Read me, over."
The kitchen now a vortex held its breath
And waited for the ways of wind and ice.
"Wind northeast, heavy packed ice,
Moving twenty knots,
Large patch of seals, southeast Cape John."
The names of ships now heading for the patch...
The *Algerine*, the *Harp*, the *Hood*.

Soon men came in through kitchen doors
And took their place on chairs they sat for years
And yearned and yarned about the flow of ice,
How long it took the seals to come to shore.
The keeper moved with horn and light
Amidst the wind and darkness
And then he broke the silence in the storm:
"Taking seals off Twillingate, Long Point."
Now he had us in the fray.
For some it was to the Wadhams, but too far for us.
Soon news of seals off Western Head
Hauled men from roads and kitchens
And with haulin' rope and gaff
Trod upon the sea and ice.
The shadows of the keeper's light
The music of his horn.

MOON ON THIRD POND

for Howard Gillingham

Your red body
Rose out of the Wadham Sea
And travelled to the quagmires
Of the upper Gander.
Standing among the hoar frost
Of the river's bank,
Two people transfixed by your resurrection
Listening to your silence
And the ghostly sounds
Of wrenching ice.
Did you see the first peoples to stand here, O Moon,
The skins of their ochre bodies
A reflection of you tonight
Making their way among the tide rips,
Among the sish ice of early fall?
Do you remember
When you last saw the smoke
From their houses,
Heard the haunting music
From their burial grounds?
The rivermen still carry their stories
Among the 'rattles' and 'steadies'
As they extract trees from the forest
And give them to the tides of the river
To erect their own tenements,
The St. John's traders
And those of London and New York.

Not bad for you dear river,
But you O Moon,
Did you see the workers' wounded hands,
Their scared faces,
Their lifeless bodies hauled
From the depths of the river?
Did you hear the rumble
From their stomachs,
Their crying children,
Hungry, cold,
Their women seeking the help of angels
When no love came
Until the river gave up their men
To start the cycle of love and children
One more time?
How can you be so stoic O Moon?
Do you remember the virgin stands
Of pine, birch and black spruce
Among which men wandered their trails,
Safe and dignified,
At one with the earth and the sky?
And now they shed tears
In the naked loneliness
Left by the savage machines
Of the day and of the night.
The earth weeps,
The river is scared.

You have told us much about love O Moon,
About the tides,
Planting our gardens,
The slaughter of animals.
Tell us about the forest, O Moon,
Or would you rather smile at our vulgarity?

THE MAN WHO BROUGHT THE HOOPS

Your lineage stretched throughout Fridays Bay
Where the land and sea
Caressed the souls of your people
As they worked the lumberwoods,
Sweating under the hot sun of summer
And the heavy frosts of winter,
Hauling the blades of bucksaws
For ninety-cents a cord...
Pit prop for the mines of America,
And paper for the law firms
Of London and New York.
Our leaders struggled
To keep your back bent,
To keep your voice hushed throughout the forest
While they filled the boards of the paper makers
With their stooges to keep you silent.
But amidst broken backs
And hands that could no longer feel
The touch of love,
They could not silence your spirit.
To feed the mouths of your withered
Sons and daughters
You cut tant trees of birch and maple,
Cut on your own time,
And in your workplace, made hoops
Forging the perfect circle,
The smells of marlin drifting out
To Muddy Hole and Trump Island.

Then like new clothes at Easter
You eased your frail body inside the circle,
Bundle after bundle,
Leaving enough room for your legs
To make the seven mile journey
Through the forest
To the merchant's room,
Earning two dollar bills
To bind the staves of the fish casks,
To wrap the salt cod
For Lisbon, Madrid and Jamaica.

THE COOPER

You plied your trade on the merchant's room
Making fish casks in the cooper shop,
Often alone,
Among the staves and shavins,
The smells of oakum,
The sounds of a morning fire.
The movements of your body
Synchronized with the implements
Of your trade...
Your mallets, irons and crozin' planes,
Emitting their own tunes
As your worn hands
Spawned a new cask
In the middle of nowhere
And slowly glided it
To meet the flames in the flume,
To bend the staves,
To give the oval shape
For the hoops to hold the staves,
To hold the fish.
With your long arms
You swung the half-moon plane
Back and forth
Among the tops of the staves,
Honing the perfect groove.
With iron and mallet
You wrapped the body of the cask
In the nish hoops of autumn.

After men packed fish among the frosts of fall
Your concerto was complete,
Swinging irons and mallets
On barrel heads and hoops,
Stencils validating
The cure of cod,
The art of those who made the fish.
Fifty years ago you played
Your last tune,
Stoic, without pension or praise,
The tools of your trade silenced
By the new bourgeoisie.

ODE TO THE JUNIPER
for Gerry Squires

O Juniper, (*Juniperus communis*)
You've had many vying
For your name;
Tamarack, Larch leaching
Unto your progeny,
Pretending to be you.
But you retain your dignity
Around the boglands
Where no other tree
Dares to grow,
Your back carrying the burden
Of the west wind
Your silk, saffron needles
Weaving a silhouette
In the autumn,
A warm and tender green
In summer,
With winter weaving its icicles
Like molten glass
Around your buds and branches.
You've had a hard time
In the age of new medicine,
Demeaning the knowledge
Of our ancestors,
Turning our backs on
Your bark and berries,
On the beers from your boughs,

The soothing salves from your soul.
For centuries craftsmen worked
With your granite wood
Holding the sails of schooners,
The bows and bedding of boats,
The beams of slides in winter.
But in our nefarious world
We ignore you
As we devour the forest
And feast on the earth
That was your fodder.
Let's make you into a shrine
Offering up prayers of adoration,
For if you leave us,
The birds will miss your
Blanket of moldow
Hanging its emerald fabric
Among the forest.

OCTOBER JOURNEY

In memory of my father, Lloyd Durning Small, 1908-1960

The October sea was calm,
The trees as still as tombstones
While I, with heavy heart,
Walked through the forest
To Beachy Cove,
To the sights and sounds of an ancient world
That was once mine...
A maple ending her display of the season,
The juniper guarding the boglands,
Birds singing their songs of relapse and renewal,
Praying that man will not find them.
Easier now to ignore yesterday's universe
Than confront the kaleidoscope of images...
Horses hauling their heavy loads
Their bells an octave
In the morning frost
While my father studied trees for timber.
What now, with horses gone?
The landscape leaching with rust
From man's new machines,
The boglands weeping in their discontent
While blueberry bushes blush
In their embarrassment.
The gardens where men and women
Grew their winter's food
With only nature's help,
And cut grasses
And after-grasses

For animals that fed them
And clothed them
And gave them peace.
The hayfields, spread from east to west
Where once I followed horse and mower
And watched the death of grass and flowers,
Where birds now sing,
And mind their own mindful business.
The fields of ferns,
Appeared like apparitions
As slow frames of plumboys
Moved between grass and fern,
Where half-century ago
Young hands held their beauty
And morning mouths extinguished their lives.
The lily of the valley,
Holding the face of love in its cocoon,
Now bedded down for winter.
The beach in Haulin' Cove
Where I used to play with the sea
Before happiness was hostage
To the stock exchange;
Where my father's brothers
Contemplated the battlefields of Europe,
Where my father threw cast nets
In a perfect circle
Around caplin seeking their own emancipation,

Their own renewal.
Just above high tide,
The withered relics of a capstan
Where my grandfather and his sons,
With the strength from lean bodies
Gave safe harbour to their boats.
Across the water,
The two Wild Coves.
One where Jacob,
The cobbler and philosopher lived;
The other where Rich,
The kind and gentle farmer
Tended his fields
And fed his animals and family
With the glee and gracefulness
Of a humanity no longer with us.
It was lonely here with them gone
For they were so much a part
Of the mosaic
That gave meaning to our lives.
I searched for remnants of house and barn
Where men, women and animals
Intermingled in morning suns,
Where grasses bent with heavy dews
And mornings of snows
And evenings when sheep and cows
Came for human calls

And from the barn came calls
Of cows and sheep and horses,
In March the cry of lambs.
Gathered among the grasses,
Greying wood
That fifty years ago
Embraced a household
Where men manned milking stools
And women beat on butter churns
In rhythm with the rote of the sea.
Now their music gone
And I mesmerized by my memories
And the meanness of man's mortality.
A foundering ice house
Among the rocks and trees,
The builder moved to Massachusetts
To work with wood,
The arctic freeze without a chance
To chill the air of summer.
Only the sounds of the gentle sea
Broke the silence on the beach.
Berths that fished for centuries,
Without their boats and traps
Where crews hauled twine
And twisted and turned their bodies
With the weight of fish
And now, like them,

The names of berths and grounds
Are withering from the sea.
Back up the beach
The blackened rocks
From fires that roasted fish
And boiled the teas
That always had the taste of truth.
Among the trees,
A trail my father took
Weighed down with caplin for the ground
Set out from east to west.
I crept among the tomes of trees,
Transparent in their glee
That we had gone,
For now the beavers and the birds
Bade me farewell,
A requiem that was mine
And theirs,
The silence said good-bye.

TIZZARD'S HARBOUR HOMESTEAD

Yours was the last homestead
On the road to French Point
And outside of Bethlehem,
A barn worthy of the nativity.
Here calves saw their first light
And horses gave birth to yarry foals.
There were mangers and milking stools
And milk pans held by the warm hands
Of the mother of the household.

Entering by the back door
One passed porches and pantries
And always the immutable milk room
Where wooden tables held pans of fresh milk.
The kitchen table
Always surrounded by people,
Whose large and worn hands
Stretched out among the bowls of food,
Raised by men and women
Working the gardens and grasslands
All the days of their long lives.
To waiting girls and boys
Mrs. Osmond gave the elixir
Of fresh bread laden with butter,
Molasses and cream.
Then she gave a glass of milk.
In those days we believed in god,
We believed in the devil too,
But he never entered Mrs. Osmond's kitchen.

In the austere silence of Sunday afternoons
Aged men entered the large kitchen with only a nod.
All afternoon they sat chewing tobacco, smoking pipes,
With tired backs bent, elbows resting on worn knees
Making cryptic remarks
About the weather, fish and horses.
As the sun slipped into the evening sea
Those revered men from Virgil's world
Wandered home without reproof.

Today your holy house
Has gone from the landscape
And you and all the people
Who gathered in your name
Wander as ghosts in the dark night.

THIS HOUSE MUST GET LONELY AT TIMES
for Clyde Rose

You must get lonely here
By yourself
Most of the year.
No friend to listen to motors
Pushing boats
Up and down the Arm.
No one to watch the mountains,
Watching the world...
To observe the bodies of men
Moving with precision,
Back and forth
In their home on the water
As they scun twine
Throughout the days
Of the long sun
And then as the days close
And they confront the darkness
Of their lives,
They stand and sit and talk.
It is their benediction,
Theirs alone.
I am guilty of listening to them
From an upstairs window.
But blessed house
You can't be charged with guilt;
It is your business to be vigil,
For we have deserted you.

Don't be afraid to watch
The changing leaves by yourself,
And on Christmas Eve
And the Sixth,
And all the holy days of your life,
Sing for us
And we will listen.

CHRISTMAS

Christmas is only five days old
And I am already lonely.
The earth has new snow.
The sky,
Patches of white and blue,
Sending shades of light on hills
That are not mine.
But it is in the language of
Light and darkness on the landscape
That I look for the symbols of solitude
That once made all days special,
Especially Christmas.
The men and women who gave meaning
To the season
Have vacated their homesteads
In search of the final solitude;
Their houses fading from the landscape
Or filled with strangers.
I have no place to go.
I am left with my memories,
Telling stories to men and women
Who do not know my people.

DEATH OF A PEOPLE
for Des Walsh

Like the call of the loon
In the autumn
The names rang out...
Emmanual, Ephriam, Joseph,
Jabez, Reuben, William.
Time took its toll
And the men and women who carried
The memories of genesis,
Of land and church and cemeteries,
Of stages and stores,
Of bawns and trapberths,
They left us a long time ago.
And now you, Arthur,
Gone to rest with your people.
It was strange seeing you,
The last of my father's generation
Lying at the front of the church,
Only a few feet from where
Your ancestors stood for
Two hundred years,
Where you stood with your brothers and sisters,
Your aged mother,
Swaying back and forth
With the long hymns
Of the day and of the night.
Now those voices are silent
And there's no one left to ask
About our place,
About our people.

www.ingramcontent.com/pod-product-compliance
Lightning Source LLC
LaVergne TN
LVHW091209080426
835509LV00006B/901